EMMANUEL JOSEPH

gods and Geometry, The Intersection of Myth, Medicine, and Built Spaces

Copyright © 2025 by Emmanuel Joseph

All rights reserved. No part of this publication may be reproduced, stored or transmitted in any form or by any means, electronic, mechanical, photocopying, recording, scanning, or otherwise without written permission from the publisher. It is illegal to copy this book, post it to a website, or distribute it by any other means without permission.

First edition

This book was professionally typeset on Reedsy.
Find out more at reedsy.com

Contents

1. Chapter 1: Introduction to Myth and Geometry — 1
2. Chapter 2: Sacred Spaces and Geometric Precision — 3
3. Chapter 3: Medicine and Sacred Geometry — 5
4. Chapter 4: Mythological Narratives in Built Spaces — 7
5. Chapter 5: Geometry in Religious Iconography — 10
6. Chapter 6: The Healing Power of Geometric Design — 12
7. Chapter 7: Urban Planning and the Sacred Geometry of Cities — 15
8. Chapter 8: Symbolism in Geometric Architecture — 17
9. Chapter 9: The Influence of Geometry on Art and Design — 20
10. Chapter 10: Geometry and Cosmology in Ancient Cultures — 22
11. Chapter 11: Geometry and Ritual in Built Spaces — 24
12. Chapter 12: The Legacy of Sacred Geometry — 27

1

Chapter 1: Introduction to Myth and Geometry

In the ancient world, myths served as both cautionary tales and vessels of knowledge, blending the celestial with the terrestrial. Geometry, in its own right, traced paths from the infinite expanse of the heavens to the minutiae of earthly life. Together, these two disciplines forged a symbiotic relationship where the abstract met the tangible, providing humanity with a framework to comprehend the world around them. This chapter delves into the origins of myths and the fundamental principles of geometry, exploring how these two seemingly disparate fields converged. The intertwining of mythology and geometry offers a unique lens through which to view the ancients' understanding of their environment.

Geometry's roots extend deep into early civilizations, with the Egyptians and Babylonians laying the groundwork for mathematical concepts that would later be refined by the Greeks. The Egyptians, for instance, harnessed geometric principles to construct their monumental pyramids, which still stand as testament to their engineering prowess. These structures were not mere tombs but profound expressions of the Egyptians' cosmology and their reverence for the afterlife. In parallel, mythological narratives like those of Osiris and Isis imbued these physical spaces with divine significance, creating a seamless blend of the sacred and the scientific.

The Greeks, inheriting this rich tradition, further developed geometric principles and imbued them with philosophical significance. Philosophers such as Pythagoras and Plato saw geometry as a bridge between the physical and metaphysical realms. Pythagoras, in particular, believed that numbers and geometric forms held the key to understanding the universe's underlying order. His famous theorem, while a mathematical statement, also resonated with deeper philosophical implications about harmony and proportion in nature and the cosmos. This chapter will explore how these early geometrical insights were not just mathematical discoveries but also reflections of the ancients' quest to decipher the divine order.

In this intersection of myth and geometry, we uncover a tapestry of human thought that spans millennia. Through myths, the ancients encoded their understanding of natural phenomena, societal norms, and cosmological beliefs. Geometry provided the tools to physically manifest these concepts, whether in the form of monumental architecture or the precise layout of cities. As we journey through this chapter, we'll uncover the profound ways in which myths and geometry converged to shape not just the built environment but also the very fabric of ancient society's worldview.

2

Chapter 2: Sacred Spaces and Geometric Precision

Sacred spaces in ancient civilizations were meticulously designed to reflect the divine order and cosmic principles. Temples, shrines, and other religious structures were not only places of worship but also embodiments of the culture's understanding of the universe. Geometry played a crucial role in their construction, ensuring that every element was proportionate and harmonious. This chapter examines how different cultures used geometric principles to design sacred spaces that resonated with their mythological and spiritual beliefs.

In Ancient Egypt, the construction of temples and pyramids followed precise geometric guidelines that aligned with the stars and cardinal points. The Great Pyramid of Giza, for example, is a marvel of geometric accuracy, with its base forming a nearly perfect square. The alignment of the pyramids with the constellation Orion was intended to reflect the Egyptians' belief in the afterlife and the journey of the soul to the stars. These structures were not just tombs but cosmic gateways, designed to guide the deceased pharaohs to their divine destiny.

The Greeks, too, placed great emphasis on geometric precision in their sacred architecture. The Parthenon in Athens is a prime example of how the Greeks used geometry to create aesthetically pleasing and harmonious structures. The use of the golden ratio in its design ensured that every element of the Parthenon was proportionate, reflecting the Greek belief in balance and harmony. The temple was dedicated to Athena, the goddess of wisdom and war, and its geometric precision was seen as a reflection of her divine nature.

In India, the concept of Vastu Shastra governed the design of sacred spaces. This ancient architectural science emphasized the importance of geometric alignment and proportionality in building temples and homes. Vastu Shastra was based on the belief that the physical environment could influence spiritual and physical well-being. Temples built according to Vastu principles were designed to harmonize with cosmic energies, ensuring that worshippers experienced a sense of peace and spiritual fulfillment.

Across different cultures, the use of geometry in designing sacred spaces underscores the universal human desire to connect with the divine. Whether through the alignment of pyramids with the stars, the use of the golden ratio in Greek temples, or the principles of Vastu Shastra in Indian architecture, geometry provided a tangible means to manifest spiritual beliefs in the physical world. This chapter highlights how these sacred spaces, designed with geometric precision, served as bridges between the earthly and the divine.

3

Chapter 3: Medicine and Sacred Geometry

The ancient world often viewed medicine and healing through a lens that blended spiritual beliefs with empirical practices. Sacred geometry, with its emphasis on harmony and balance, played a significant role in the development of early medical theories and practices. This chapter explores how geometric principles informed the understanding of the human body and influenced the design of healing spaces and tools.

Hippocrates, known as the father of medicine, believed that the human body was a microcosm of the universe. He posited that health was a state of balance between the body's four humors: blood, phlegm, yellow bile, and black bile. The balance and harmony central to sacred geometry found a parallel in this medical theory, where illness was seen as a result of disharmony within the body. Hippocrates' approach to medicine emphasized the importance of natural healing and the body's ability to restore balance, reflecting the geometric principles of proportion and equilibrium.

In ancient China, the practice of acupuncture was deeply rooted in the concept of balancing the body's vital energy, or qi. The meridians, or pathways through which qi flowed, were mapped out using precise geometric patterns. These patterns were believed to correspond to the body's internal organs and functions. Acupuncture, therefore, was not just a physical intervention but a way to harmonize the body's energies, restoring health and well-being. The geometric precision in mapping the meridians highlights the ancient Chinese belief in the interconnectedness of the body and the cosmos.

The architectural design of healing spaces also reflected the influence of sacred geometry. In ancient Greece, the Asclepieion of Epidaurus was a sanctuary dedicated to Asclepius, the god of healing. The layout of the sanctuary followed geometric principles, with a central courtyard surrounded by buildings arranged in harmonious proportions. Patients would undergo various treatments, including hydrotherapy and dream interpretation, within this geometrically precise environment. The belief was that the sacred geometry of the space would facilitate healing by aligning the patient's energies with the divine order.

Similarly, in ancient India, the design of Ayurvedic healing centers was influenced by the principles of Vastu Shastra. These centers were built to harmonize with the natural environment, creating a sense of balance and tranquility that was conducive to healing. The geometric alignment of buildings and the use of specific materials were believed to enhance the flow of positive energy, promoting physical and spiritual well-being.

This chapter highlights the profound ways in which sacred geometry informed the practice of medicine in ancient civilizations. By blending spiritual beliefs with empirical practices, these cultures created a holistic approach to healing that emphasized balance, harmony, and the interconnectedness of the body and the cosmos.

4

Chapter 4: Mythological Narratives in Built Spaces

Mythological narratives have always played a crucial role in shaping the built environment. Ancient civilizations often embedded their myths and legends into the very fabric of their cities and monuments. This chapter explores how mythological stories influenced the design and construction of built spaces, creating environments that were rich with symbolic meaning and cultural significance.

In Ancient Greece, the city of Athens was deeply intertwined with the myth of Athena, the goddess of wisdom and war. The Parthenon, one of the most iconic structures in the city, was dedicated to her and symbolized her protection over the city. The friezes and sculptures adorning the Parthenon depicted scenes from Greek mythology, celebrating the gods and heroes who were believed to influence the city's fate. These mythological narratives were not just decorative elements but integral to the identity and function of the built spaces.

Similarly, in ancient Rome, the myth of Romulus and Remus, the twin founders of the city, was reflected in the architecture and layout of the city. The Roman Forum, the political and religious heart of Rome, was designed to embody the myth of the city's divine origins. The temples and public buildings within the Forum were adorned with sculptures and reliefs depicting scenes from Roman mythology, reinforcing the belief in the gods' active involvement in the city's affairs. The architecture of Rome thus became a physical manifestation of its mythological heritage.

In ancient Egypt, the construction of temples and pyramids was deeply influenced by mythological narratives. The temple of Horus at Edfu, for instance, was designed to reflect the myth of Horus and his battle with Seth. The layout and decoration of the temple followed the storyline of the myth, guiding worshippers through the narrative as they moved through the space. These built spaces served as both places of worship and storytelling mediums, preserving and transmitting the culture's myths and legends.

The influence of mythological narratives on built spaces is also evident in ancient Mesoamerican civilizations. The city of Teotihuacan, for example, was designed with a central avenue known as the Avenue of the Dead, lined with monumental structures such as the Pyramid of the Sun and the Pyramid of the Moon. These pyramids were believed to be sacred spaces where the gods interacted with the human world. The alignment of the city with celestial events and the incorporation of mythological symbolism in its architecture were integral to the spiritual and cultural life of the inhabitants. The myth of Quetzalcoatl, the feathered serpent god, played a central role in the city's design. The Pyramid of the Sun, for example, was aligned with the setting sun during the summer solstice, reflecting the mythological belief in the connection between the divine and the natural world. These built spaces were more than just physical structures; they were embodiments of the culture's myths and spiritual beliefs.

In ancient India, the epics of the Mahabharata and the Ramayana influenced the design and construction of temples and other sacred spaces. The stories of gods, heroes, and their exploits were often depicted in intricate carvings and sculptures on temple walls. The temple of Angkor Wat in Cambodia, dedicated to the Hindu god Vishnu, is a prime example of this practice. The temple's design and decoration are deeply rooted in Hindu mythology, with bas-reliefs depicting scenes from the Mahabharata and the Ramayana. These mythological narratives were not only artistic expressions but also served to educate and inspire the faithful.

CHAPTER 4: MYTHOLOGICAL NARRATIVES IN BUILT SPACES

The integration of mythological narratives into built spaces provided a way for ancient civilizations to preserve and transmit their cultural heritage. These spaces were living embodiments of the myths and legends that shaped the identity and beliefs of the people. By embedding these stories into their architecture, ancient cultures ensured that their myths would be remembered and revered for generations to come. This chapter highlights the profound influence of mythological narratives on the design and construction of built spaces, creating environments that were rich with symbolic meaning and cultural significance.

5

Chapter 5: Geometry in Religious Iconography

Religious iconography has always been a powerful means of conveying spiritual and mythological themes. Geometry, with its emphasis on harmony and proportion, played a crucial role in the creation of religious symbols and artwork. This chapter explores how geometric principles influenced the design of religious iconography in various cultures, creating symbols that were not only visually striking but also deeply meaningful.

In Christianity, the use of geometric shapes and patterns is evident in the design of churches, cathedrals, and religious artwork. The rose windows of Gothic cathedrals, for example, are masterpieces of geometric design. These intricate stained glass windows, with their circular patterns and symmetrical designs, symbolize the divine order and the beauty of creation. The use of the circle, a shape with no beginning or end, represents the eternal nature of God. The geometric precision in these designs reflects the belief in the harmony and perfection of the divine.

In Islamic art, the use of geometric patterns is a defining feature. Islamic religious iconography avoids the depiction of human figures, focusing instead on abstract geometric designs and intricate arabesques. These patterns, known as tessellations, are created using precise mathematical principles and reflect the Islamic belief in the infinite nature of God. The geometric complexity of these designs serves as a reminder of the divine presence in all aspects of life. The use of symmetry and repetition in Islamic art creates a sense of unity and order, reflecting the spiritual ideals of the faith.

In Hinduism, geometric patterns known as mandalas are used in religious iconography and rituals. Mandalas are complex geometric designs that represent the universe and the divine. They are used as tools for meditation and spiritual growth, helping practitioners to focus their minds and connect with the divine. The intricate patterns and symmetrical designs of mandalas symbolize the interconnectedness of all things and the underlying order of the cosmos. The geometric precision in these designs reflects the Hindu belief in the harmony and balance of the universe.

The use of geometry in religious iconography is a testament to the universal human desire to connect with the divine. By incorporating geometric principles into their religious symbols and artwork, cultures around the world have created powerful expressions of their spiritual beliefs. This chapter highlights the role of geometry in the creation of religious iconography, revealing the deep connection between the visual and the spiritual.

6

Chapter 6: The Healing Power of Geometric Design

Throughout history, geometric design has been used to create spaces that promote physical and spiritual well-being. The ancient belief in the healing power of geometry is evident in the design of temples, gardens, and other spaces intended for healing and contemplation. This chapter explores how different cultures harnessed the principles of geometry to create environments that fostered health and harmony.

In ancient Egypt, the design of healing spaces was closely tied to the concept of Ma'at, the principle of cosmic order and balance. Temples dedicated to healing gods such as Imhotep were designed to embody the principles of Ma'at, with precise geometric layouts and harmonious proportions. The temples served as sanctuaries where patients could seek both physical and spiritual healing. The alignment of the temples with celestial events and natural landmarks was believed to enhance their healing power, connecting the patients with the divine order of the universe.

In ancient Greece, the Asclepieia, or healing sanctuaries dedicated to Asclepius, the god of medicine, were designed to promote healing through their geometric precision and natural beauty. The Asclepieion of Epidaurus, for example, featured a central courtyard surrounded by buildings arranged in harmonious proportions. Patients would undergo various treatments,

CHAPTER 6: THE HEALING POWER OF GEOMETRIC DESIGN

including hydrotherapy and dream interpretation, within this carefully designed environment. The belief was that the geometric harmony of the space would facilitate healing by aligning the patient's energies with the divine order.

In Chinese medicine, the design of healing spaces was influenced by the principles of feng shui, which emphasizes the importance of harmony and balance in the environment. Feng shui practitioners use geometric principles to create spaces that promote the flow of positive energy, or qi, and enhance physical and spiritual well-being. The layout of buildings, the placement of furniture, and the use of specific colors and materials are all carefully considered to create a harmonious and healing environment.

In Japan, the design of Zen gardens reflects the belief in the healing power of geometric design. These carefully arranged gardens use rocks, sand, and plants to create simple yet profound geometric patterns that promote meditation and inner peace. The design of Zen gardens is based on the principles of harmony, balance, and simplicity, creating spaces that foster spiritual growth and well-being.

The use of geometric design in healing spaces highlights the ancient belief in the connection between the physical and the spiritual. By creating environments that embody the principles of geometry, cultures around the world have sought to promote health, harmony, and spiritual well-being. This chapter explores the healing power of geometric design, revealing how ancient cultures harnessed the principles of geometry to create spaces that nurtured both body and soul.

The ancient belief in the healing power of geometry is further reflected in the design of sacred groves and gardens in various cultures. In ancient Greece, the groves dedicated to the gods were carefully cultivated spaces that provided a tranquil environment for reflection and healing. These groves were often designed with geometric layouts, incorporating pathways, fountains, and statues that created a harmonious and aesthetically pleasing atmosphere. The belief was that the geometric design of these spaces could enhance the spiritual and physical well-being of those who visited them.

In Islamic culture, the concept of the chaharbagh, or four-part garden, is a prime example of the use of geometric design in creating healing environments. The chaharbagh is divided into four quadrants by water channels, symbolizing the four rivers of paradise mentioned in the Quran. The geometric precision of the chaharbagh's layout creates a sense of balance and order, reflecting the Islamic belief in the harmony of the cosmos. These gardens served as places of contemplation and relaxation, where visitors could connect with the divine and experience a sense of inner peace.

The use of geometric design in healing spaces continues to be relevant in modern architecture and urban planning. Hospitals, for example, are often designed with geometric principles in mind to create environments that promote healing and well-being. The layout of patient rooms, the use of natural light, and the incorporation of green spaces are all carefully considered to create a healing environment. The belief in the healing power of geometry is reflected in the design of these spaces, where the principles of harmony and balance continue to guide the creation of environments that nurture both body and soul.

This chapter highlights the enduring belief in the healing power of geometric design, revealing how ancient cultures harnessed the principles of geometry to create spaces that fostered health and harmony. From sacred groves and gardens to modern hospitals, the use of geometric design in healing environments underscores the timeless connection between the physical and the spiritual.

7

Chapter 7: Urban Planning and the Sacred Geometry of Cities

The design and layout of cities have always been influenced by both practical considerations and spiritual beliefs. Ancient civilizations often used geometric principles to plan their cities, creating urban environments that reflected their cosmological views and cultural values. This chapter explores how different cultures incorporated sacred geometry into their urban planning, shaping the built environment in ways that resonated with their spiritual and mythological beliefs.

In ancient Egypt, the city of Thebes was a prime example of how sacred geometry influenced urban planning. The city's layout was aligned with the Nile River and the cardinal points, reflecting the Egyptians' belief in the cosmic order. The temples of Karnak and Luxor, situated on the east bank of the Nile, were designed with precise geometric proportions and aligned with celestial events. The processional avenue connecting the two temples was flanked by rows of sphinxes, symbolizing the pharaoh's divine protection. The geometric precision of Thebes' layout created a harmonious environment that embodied the Egyptians' spiritual beliefs.

The ancient Greeks also used geometric principles in their urban planning. The city of Miletus, designed by the architect Hippodamus, is considered one of the earliest examples of planned urban design. Hippodamus's plan for Miletus was based on a grid layout, with streets intersecting at right angles to create a series of rectangular blocks. This geometric design facilitated efficient movement and organization within the city, reflecting the Greek belief in order and rationality. The incorporation of public spaces such as agoras, theatres, and temples within the geometric layout created a harmonious environment that supported the social and spiritual life of the city.

In ancient India, the city of Jaipur was designed according to the principles of Vastu Shastra, the ancient science of architecture. The city's layout followed a precise geometric plan, with streets and buildings aligned to the cardinal points. The city was divided into nine rectangular sectors, each representing a specific aspect of life and the cosmos. The central sector, which housed the royal palace and temples, was considered the heart of the city. The geometric precision of Jaipur's layout was believed to create a balanced and harmonious environment that promoted prosperity and well-being.

The influence of sacred geometry on urban planning is also evident in the design of ancient Mesoamerican cities. The city of Tenochtitlan, the capital of the Aztec Empire, was built on an island in the middle of Lake Texcoco. The city's layout was based on a grid plan, with a central plaza surrounded by temples, palaces, and public buildings. The Templo Mayor, the main temple of Tenochtitlan, was aligned with the cardinal points and dedicated to the gods Huitzilopochtli and Tlaloc. The geometric precision of Tenochtitlan's layout reflected the Aztec belief in the interconnectedness of the earthly and divine realms.

This chapter highlights the role of sacred geometry in the urban planning of ancient civilizations, revealing how geometric principles were used to create harmonious and spiritually resonant environments. By incorporating sacred geometry into their city designs, these cultures created urban environments that reflected their cosmological views and cultural values, shaping the built environment in profound and lasting ways.

8

Chapter 8: Symbolism in Geometric Architecture

Geometric shapes and patterns have always been imbued with symbolic meaning, reflecting the cultural and spiritual beliefs of the societies that created them. This chapter explores the symbolic significance of geometric architecture in various cultures, revealing how shapes and patterns were used to convey deep cultural and spiritual messages.

In ancient Egypt, the pyramid is one of the most iconic examples of geometric architecture. The pyramid's triangular shape symbolized the rays of the sun, connecting the pharaohs with the sun god Ra. The pyramid's four sides, which converge at a single point, also represented the concept of unity and the pharaoh's divine authority over the four corners of the earth. The geometric precision of the pyramids, with their perfectly aligned sides and angles, reflected the Egyptians' belief in cosmic order and harmony.

In Islamic architecture, the use of geometric patterns is a defining feature. The intricate tessellations and arabesques that adorn mosques and other religious buildings are created using precise mathematical principles. These geometric patterns symbolize the infinite nature of God and the underlying order of the universe. The use of symmetry and repetition in Islamic art creates a sense of unity and balance, reflecting the spiritual ideals of the faith. The geometric precision of these designs serves as a visual reminder of the divine presence in all aspects of life.

In Hinduism, the mandala is a powerful symbol of geometric architecture. Mandalas are complex geometric designs that represent the universe and the divine. They are used as tools for meditation and spiritual growth, helping practitioners to focus their minds and connect with the divine. The intricate patterns and symmetrical designs of mandalas symbolize the interconnectedness of all things and the underlying order of the cosmos. The geometric precision of these designs reflects the Hindu belief in the harmony and balance of the universe.

In Chinese culture, the use of geometric shapes and patterns in architecture is closely tied to the principles of feng shui. The design of buildings and spaces is carefully considered to create a harmonious flow of energy, or qi. Geometric shapes such as circles, squares, and hexagons are used to create balanced and harmonious environments. The use of symmetry and proportion in Chinese architecture reflects the belief in the interconnectedness of the physical and spiritual realms. The geometric precision of these designs enhances the flow of positive energy, promoting health and well-being.

The use of geometric architecture as a medium for symbolic expression extends beyond the cultures we've explored. In the Americas, the ancient Maya civilization is renowned for its sophisticated use of geometry in architectural design. The Pyramid of Kukulcán at Chichén Itzá, also known as El Castillo, is a striking example of geometric symbolism. This pyramid not only served as a temple but also as a calendar. During the equinoxes, the setting sun casts shadows on the pyramid's steps, creating the illusion of a serpent slithering down the structure. This phenomenon symbolizes the descent of the feathered serpent god, Kukulcán, blending mythology with geometric precision.

The Gothic cathedrals of medieval Europe are another testament to the symbolic power of geometric architecture. These cathedrals were designed with intricate geometric patterns, including pointed arches, ribbed vaults, and flying buttresses, which allowed for the construction of towering structures with large stained-glass windows. The rose windows, often placed at the center of the cathedral's facade, are masterpieces of geometric design. The

CHAPTER 8: SYMBOLISM IN GEOMETRIC ARCHITECTURE

circular pattern symbolizes the divine, with its intricate tracery representing the complexity and beauty of creation. The geometric precision of these cathedrals reflects the medieval belief in the order and harmony of the universe.

In Japan, the traditional tea house is a prime example of geometric symbolism in architecture. The design of the tea house follows the principles of wabi-sabi, which emphasizes simplicity, humility, and the beauty of imperfection. The layout of the tea house is based on geometric proportions, creating a harmonious and serene environment. The use of natural materials, such as wood and bamboo, enhances the connection to nature, while the geometric design reflects the Japanese belief in balance and harmony. The tea house serves as a space for the traditional tea ceremony, a ritual that embodies the principles of mindfulness and spiritual refinement.

The incorporation of geometric symbolism in architecture is a reflection of the universal human desire to connect with the divine and express cultural values. By using geometric shapes and patterns, ancient cultures created built spaces that were not only functional but also deeply meaningful. This chapter highlights the enduring power of geometric architecture as a medium for symbolic expression, revealing the profound ways in which shapes and patterns have shaped the built environment throughout history.

9

Chapter 9: The Influence of Geometry on Art and Design

The principles of geometry have not only influenced architecture but also permeated various forms of art and design. This chapter explores how geometric principles have been applied in the visual arts, from ancient pottery and textiles to modern abstract art, revealing the timeless connection between geometry and creativity.

In ancient Greece, the use of geometric patterns in pottery and ceramics is a prominent feature of the Geometric period (900-700 BCE). Pottery from this era is adorned with intricate patterns of circles, triangles, and meanders, reflecting the Greek appreciation for order and symmetry. These geometric motifs were not only decorative but also conveyed symbolic meaning, often associated with fertility, protection, and the cycles of nature. The precision and complexity of these designs demonstrate the Greek mastery of geometric principles and their application in everyday objects.

In Islamic art, the use of geometric patterns is a defining characteristic. The intricate tilework, mosaics, and calligraphy found in Islamic architecture are created using precise geometric principles. The repetition and symmetry of these patterns reflect the Islamic belief in the infinite nature of God and the underlying order of the universe. Geometric design is also evident in Islamic textiles and carpets, where complex patterns are woven into the fabric,

CHAPTER 9: THE INFLUENCE OF GEOMETRY ON ART AND DESIGN

creating visually stunning and spiritually meaningful works of art.

The influence of geometry on art is also evident in the Renaissance, a period marked by a renewed interest in the mathematical principles of ancient Greece and Rome. Artists such as Leonardo da Vinci and Albrecht Dürer used geometric principles to create works of art that were both scientifically accurate and aesthetically pleasing. Da Vinci's Vitruvian Man, for example, is a study of human proportions based on geometric principles, reflecting the Renaissance belief in the harmony between the human body and the cosmos. Dürer's engravings and woodcuts often incorporated geometric shapes and patterns, demonstrating his deep understanding of mathematical principles and their application in art.

In the modern era, the influence of geometry is evident in the works of abstract artists such as Piet Mondrian and Wassily Kandinsky. Mondrian's compositions, characterized by the use of vertical and horizontal lines and primary colors, are based on the principles of geometric abstraction. His work reflects the belief in the harmony and balance of geometric forms. Kandinsky, on the other hand, used geometric shapes and patterns to convey spiritual and emotional content, exploring the connection between form, color, and meaning. The precision and simplicity of geometric abstraction continue to inspire contemporary artists and designers, demonstrating the enduring power of geometry in the visual arts.

This chapter highlights the influence of geometric principles on various forms of art and design, revealing the timeless connection between geometry and creativity. From ancient pottery and textiles to modern abstract art, the application of geometric principles has shaped the way we create and perceive visual art, reflecting the universal human appreciation for order, symmetry, and harmony.

10

Chapter 10: Geometry and Cosmology in Ancient Cultures

The study of the cosmos has always been a central concern for human societies, and geometry has played a crucial role in understanding and representing the heavens. This chapter explores how ancient cultures used geometric principles to study the stars and planets, creating sophisticated astronomical systems that reflected their cosmological beliefs.

In ancient Mesopotamia, the Babylonians developed an advanced system of astronomy based on geometric principles. They used mathematical calculations to predict the movements of celestial bodies and created detailed star catalogs. The Babylonian ziggurats, towering structures with a series of ascending terraces, were not only religious temples but also observatories for studying the heavens. The geometric design of these structures allowed for precise observations of the stars and planets, reflecting the Babylonians' belief in the interconnectedness of the earthly and celestial realms.

In ancient Greece, the study of geometry and astronomy was deeply intertwined. The philosopher Pythagoras is credited with the discovery that the movements of celestial bodies could be described using mathematical ratios, leading to the concept of the "harmony of the spheres." This idea suggested that the planets and stars moved in harmonious orbits, creating a celestial music that could be understood through geometric principles. The

CHAPTER 10: GEOMETRY AND COSMOLOGY IN ANCIENT CULTURES

Greek astronomer Hipparchus used geometric models to map the stars and calculate the positions of celestial bodies, laying the groundwork for future astronomical discoveries.

The ancient Maya civilization also demonstrated a deep understanding of geometry and astronomy. The Maya developed a complex calendar system based on precise observations of the sun, moon, and planets. The alignment of their cities and temples with celestial events, such as solstices and equinoxes, reflected their cosmological beliefs. The Temple of Kukulcán at Chichén Itzá, for example, was designed to align with the movements of the sun, creating a visual representation of the Maya's astronomical knowledge. The geometric precision of Maya architecture and their sophisticated calendar system reveal the profound connection between geometry and cosmology in their culture.

In ancient China, the study of astronomy was closely linked to the principles of feng shui and the belief in the harmony between heaven and earth. Chinese astronomers used geometric principles to map the stars and create detailed celestial charts. The design of imperial palaces and temples often incorporated celestial alignments, reflecting the belief in the emperor's divine mandate to rule. The Forbidden City in Beijing, for example, is aligned with the cardinal points and designed according to principles that mirror the cosmic order, symbolizing the harmony between the earthly and celestial realms.

This chapter highlights the role of geometry in the study of cosmology in ancient cultures, revealing how geometric principles were used to understand and represent the heavens. By applying geometric principles to their observations of the stars and planets, these cultures created sophisticated astronomical systems that reflected their cosmological beliefs, shaping their understanding of the universe in profound ways.

11

Chapter 11: Geometry and Ritual in Built Spaces

Rituals have always been an essential aspect of human culture, and the design of spaces for ritual practices often incorporates geometric principles. This chapter explores how geometry has been used to create spaces that enhance the experience of rituals, reflecting the cultural and spiritual significance of these practices.

In ancient Greece, the design of theaters for ritual performances was based on precise geometric principles. The circular orchestra, where the chorus performed, and the tiered seating arrangement were designed to create optimal acoustics and visibility. The theater at Epidaurus is a prime example of this geometric precision, with its perfect circular orchestra and concentric seating arrangement. The geometric design of the theater enhanced the ritual experience, creating a space where the audience could engage with the performance on a deep spiritual level.

In ancient Egypt, the temples dedicated to gods and goddesses were meticulously designed to facilitate ritual practices. The layout of the temples followed a geometric plan, with a series of courtyards, halls, and sanctuaries leading to the inner sanctum, where the deity's statue was housed. The alignment of the temples with celestial events, such as the rising and setting of the sun, enhanced the spiritual significance of the rituals performed within geometric principles to enhance the spiritual experience of rituals. The layout of these shrines often includes a series of torii gates that mark the transition from the mundane world to the sacred space. The geometric alignment of these gates creates a pathway that guides worshippers towards the inner sanctum, where rituals and prayers are offered to the kami, or spirits. The use of geometry in the design of Shinto shrines reflects the Japanese belief in the harmony between nature and the spiritual world.

This chapter highlights the role of geometry in the design of ritual spaces, revealing how ancient cultures used geometric principles to create environments that enhanced the spiritual experience of rituals. By incorporating geometry into the design of their sacred spaces, these cultures created powerful settings for rituals that connected them with the divine and maintained cosmic harmony.

CHAPTER 11: GEOMETRY AND RITUAL IN BUILT SPACES

these spaces. The temple of Karnak, with its vast hypostyle hall and precise alignment with the solstices, is a testament to the geometric precision used to create spaces for ritual practices.

In Hinduism, the design of temples and the performance of rituals are closely tied to the principles of Vastu Shastra. The layout of the temples follows a geometric plan, with the central sanctum, or garbhagriha, representing the cosmic center. The use of specific proportions and alignments in the temple's design is believed to enhance the flow of spiritual energy, creating a space that is conducive to rituals and meditation. The Brihadeeswarar Temple in Tamil Nadu, with its towering vimana and precise geometric layout, is a magnificent example of how geometry is used to create sacred spaces that enhance ritual practices. The temple's design follows the principles of Vastu Shastra, with its central sanctum aligned to capture the first rays of the morning sun. The geometric patterns and proportions of the temple create a harmonious environment that supports the spiritual energy of the rituals performed within its walls.

In Mesoamerica, the design of ceremonial centers and pyramids was closely tied to the practice of rituals. The ancient city of Teotihuacan, with its Pyramid of the Sun and Pyramid of the Moon, was a major center for religious rituals and ceremonies. The alignment of the pyramids with celestial events, such as the solstices and equinoxes, reflected the Mesoamerican belief in the interconnectedness of the earthly and celestial realms. The geometric precision of these structures created a powerful setting for rituals that honored the gods and sought to maintain cosmic harmony.

The use of geometry in the design of ritual spaces is also evident in the stone circles of Neolithic Britain. Stonehenge, one of the most famous prehistoric monuments, is a prime example of geometric design used to create a space for ritual practices. The circular arrangement of the massive stones, with their precise alignment to the solstices, reflects the ancient belief in the cyclical nature of time and the importance of celestial events. The geometric layout of Stonehenge created a sacred space where rituals were performed to mark significant moments in the agricultural and solar calendar.

In the context of Japanese culture, the design of Shinto shrines incorporates

12

Chapter 12: The Legacy of Sacred Geometry

The principles of sacred geometry have left an enduring legacy that continues to influence contemporary architecture, art, and design. This chapter explores how the geometric principles developed by ancient cultures have been adapted and reinterpreted in modern times, revealing the timeless relevance of sacred geometry.

In contemporary architecture, the use of geometric principles is evident in the design of iconic buildings and structures. The Sydney Opera House, designed by architect Jørn Utzon, is a modern masterpiece that incorporates geometric forms inspired by natural shapes. The soaring roof shells, which resemble billowing sails, are created using precise mathematical calculations. The geometric design of the Opera House not only creates a visually striking structure but also enhances its acoustic properties, reflecting the harmony between form and function.

The influence of sacred geometry is also evident in the work of modern artists and designers. The paintings of Piet Mondrian, with their use of vertical and horizontal lines and primary colors, are based on the principles of geometric abstraction. Mondrian's work reflects his belief in the harmony and balance of geometric forms, creating compositions that are both visually pleasing and spiritually meaningful. The geometric patterns and designs of contemporary textile artists, such as Anni Albers, also draw on the principles of sacred geometry, creating intricate and harmonious works that resonate with ancient traditions.

In the field of urban planning, the legacy of sacred geometry is reflected in the design of sustainable and harmonious cities. The concept of the garden city, developed by urban planner Ebenezer Howard, incorporates geometric principles to create balanced and healthy urban environments. The layout of garden cities includes green spaces, public parks, and carefully planned residential areas, promoting a sense of community and well-being. The use of geometric design in urban planning reflects the timeless belief in the importance of harmony between the built environment and the natural world.

The principles of sacred geometry continue to inspire contemporary design in various fields, from architecture and art to urban planning and landscape design. The enduring legacy of sacred geometry is a testament to the timeless relevance of the geometric principles developed by ancient cultures. By incorporating these principles into modern design, we create environments that are not only visually striking but also harmonious and meaningful, reflecting the deep connection between geometry, culture, and spirituality.

This chapter concludes our exploration of the intersection of myth, medicine, and built spaces through the lens of sacred geometry. The study of sacred geometry reveals the profound ways in which ancient cultures used geometric principles to create spaces that reflected their spiritual beliefs and cultural values. From the design of temples and pyramids to the creation of intricate artworks and sustainable cities, the legacy of sacred geometry continues to shape the built environment in profound and lasting ways.

Book Description: Gods and Geometry: The Intersection of Myth, Medicine, and Built Spaces

Journey through the ancient world where myths intertwine with geometry to shape the very foundation of human civilization. In "Gods and Geometry: The Intersection of Myth, Medicine, and Built Spaces," explore how geometric principles and mythological narratives guided the construction of sacred spaces, healing centers, and urban landscapes in various cultures.

From the monumental pyramids of Egypt to the harmonious temples of

CHAPTER 12: THE LEGACY OF SACRED GEOMETRY

Greece and the intricate designs of Mesoamerican cities, this book delves into the profound relationship between geometry and the spiritual beliefs of ancient societies. Discover how geometry influenced the development of medicine, informed the design of religious iconography, and created environments that fostered health and harmony.

Through twelve captivating chapters, this book reveals the enduring legacy of sacred geometry and its impact on contemporary architecture, art, and urban planning. Whether you're fascinated by ancient history, architecture, or the mystical connection between the physical and spiritual realms, "Gods and Geometry" offers a compelling exploration of how geometric principles shaped the built environment in ways that continue to resonate today.

www.ingramcontent.com/pod-product-compliance
Lightning Source LLC
LaVergne TN
LVHW010444070526
838199LV00066B/6186